Building Dreams:

A Guide to Developing New Construction Projects

I0479248

Table of Contents

- Understanding the costs involved in building a home: Discuss the various costs associated with building a home such as land, materials, labor, permits, and fees.

- Establishing a realistic budget: Provide tips on how to create a budget that is realistic and achievable, including advice on how to account for unexpected expenses.

Chapter 4: Financing Your Dream Home

- Understanding your financing options: Explain the different financing options available for building a home, including construction loans, mortgages, and government-backed programs.

- Getting pre-approved for a mortgage: Offer advice on how to obtain pre-approval for a mortgage to help determine how much home buyers can afford.

Chapter 5: Finding a Building Site

- Identifying potential locations for your home: Offer guidance on how to choose a location for building a new home, including factors such as proximity to work, school, and amenities.

- Assessing the suitability of a building site: Discuss the importance of considering the characteristics of a building site, such as slope, soil type, and zoning regulations, to ensure it is suitable for building.

Chapter 6: Choosing a Builder

- Evaluating potential builders: Provide guidance on how to evaluate potential builders, including checking their reputation, experience, and references.

- Selecting the right builder for your project: Discuss the importance of choosing a builder who is a good fit in terms of communication style, project management, and shared vision for the project.

Chapter 7: Designing Your Home

- Working with an architect or designer: Discuss the benefits of working with a professional designer to create a custom home design that meets your needs and wants.

- Creating a custom home design: Offer guidance on the design process, including how to communicate your preferences to the designer and how to make revisions as needed.

Chapter 8: Obtaining Permits and Approvals

- Understanding the permitting process: Explain the process of obtaining permits and approvals from local authorities, including building permits, zoning permits, and environmental permits.

- Obtaining necessary approvals from local authorities: Offer advice on how to navigate the permitting process and obtain necessary approvals to move forward with construction.

Chapter 9: Preparing Your Building Site

- Clearing and grading the site: Discuss the importance of preparing the building site by clearing vegetation, grading the land, and addressing any drainage issues.

- Preparing for construction: Offer guidance on how to prepare for the start of construction, including setting up a temporary office and staging area.

Chapter 10: Building the Foundation

- Pouring the foundation: Explain the process of pouring the foundation and how to ensure it is level and strong.

- Constructing the basement or crawl space: Discuss the options for creating a basement or crawl space and the benefits of each.

Chapter 11: Framing the House

- Building the frame of the home: Explain the process of framing the house

- Types of framing: Discuss the different types of framing, such as stick framing or panelized framing, and the pros and cons of each.

- Installing windows and doors: Explain the importance of properly installing windows and doors, including energy efficiency and safety considerations.

Chapter 12: Electrical and Plumbing

- Rough-in electrical and plumbing: Explain the process of roughing in electrical and plumbing systems before the walls are closed up.

- Choosing fixtures and appliances: Offer guidance on selecting energy-efficient fixtures and appliances that fit your budget and design preferences.

Chapter 13: Insulation and Drywall

- Installing insulation: Discuss the importance of proper insulation to ensure energy efficiency and comfort.

- Hanging drywall: Explain the process of hanging drywall and how to ensure a smooth finish.

Chapter 14: Flooring, Painting, and Trim

- Installing flooring: Offer guidance on selecting flooring materials and hiring professionals to install them properly.

- Choosing paint colors: Provide advice on selecting paint colors and how to achieve a cohesive look throughout the home.

- Installing trim: Discuss the importance of proper installation of baseboards, crown molding, and other trim elements to create a finished look.

Chapter 15: Cabinets and Countertops

- Choosing cabinets: Discuss the various options for cabinetry, such as custom or prefabricated, and how to choose the best option for your needs.

- Selecting countertops: Offer guidance on selecting countertop materials, such as granite or quartz, and how to ensure proper installation.

Chapter 16: Final Touches

- Installing lighting fixtures: Discuss the importance of proper lighting and how to select fixtures that fit your style and budget.

- Landscaping: Offer guidance on landscaping the property to create a welcoming and attractive outdoor space.

Chapter 17: Final Inspections and Approvals

- Final inspections: Explain the importance of final inspections to ensure the home is safe and up to code.

- Obtaining final approvals: Discuss the process of obtaining final approvals from local authorities to ensure the home is legally compliant.

Chapter 18: Moving In

- Moving in and settling in: Offer guidance on moving in and settling into your new home, including organizing and unpacking.

Chapter 19: Maintaining Your Dream Home

- Regular maintenance tasks: Discuss the importance of regular maintenance tasks such as cleaning gutters, changing HVAC filters, and checking for leaks.

- Scheduling repairs and upgrades: Provide advice on scheduling repairs and upgrades to ensure your home remains in good condition.

Chapter 20: Conclusion

- Looking back on the process: Sum up the process of building a dream home and reflect on the rewards and challenges of the journey.

- Enjoying your dream home: Encourage readers to enjoy their new home and take pride in the accomplishment of building their dream home.

Chapter 1: Introduction to Building Your Dream Home

As an expert in the home building industry, I have had the privilege of helping countless individuals and families turn their dream of owning a custom home into a reality. Building a home from scratch can be a daunting process, but it is also one of the most rewarding experiences you can have as a homeowner. In this chapter, I will introduce you to the process of building your dream home and offer guidance on how to make your vision a reality.

1.1 Why Build Your Dream Home?

Before we dive into the details of building your dream home, it's important to understand why you might choose to build instead of buying an existing home. Here are a few reasons:

1.1.1 Customization

Building your own home allows you to have complete control over the design and layout. You can work with an architect to create a home that perfectly fits your lifestyle and aesthetic preferences.

1.1.2 Energy Efficiency

Newly constructed homes are typically much more energy-efficient than older homes. You can choose energy-efficient appliances and HVAC systems, as well as insulation and windows that help keep your home comfortable and your energy bills low.

1.1.3 Lower Maintenance Costs

When you build a new home, everything is brand new and under warranty. This means you won't have to worry about costly repairs for several years.

1.1.4 Increased Resale Value

A well-built custom home can increase in value over time, especially if you choose high-quality materials and finishes.

1.2 The Building Process

Now that we've established why building your dream home is a great option, let's dive into the process. Here are the general steps you can expect when building a custom home:

1.2.1 Design and Planning

Before construction can begin, you'll need to have a plan for your home. This involves working with an architect to create a blueprint that includes all the necessary features, such as bedrooms, bathrooms, living areas, and a kitchen. You'll also need to make decisions about materials, finishes, and other design elements.

1.2.2 Site Preparation

Once you have a plan in place, the site must be prepared for construction. This involves clearing the land, grading the site, and creating a foundation for the home.

1.2.3 Framing

The next step is to build the frame of the house. This involves constructing the walls, roof, and floor systems, which will support the weight of the home.

1.2.4 Electrical and Plumbing

After the frame is in place, the electrical and plumbing systems are roughed in. This means that the wires and pipes are installed before the walls are closed.

1.2.5 Insulation and Drywall

Once the rough-in is complete, insulation is installed to keep your home energy-efficient and comfortable. Then, drywall is hung to cover the walls.

1.2.6 Flooring, Painting, and Trim

With the walls in place, it's time to install flooring and paint the walls. Trim elements such as baseboards and crown molding are added to create a finished look.

1.2.7 Cabinets and Countertops

Kitchen and bathroom cabinets are installed, along with countertops and other fixtures.

1.2.8 Final Touches

The final touches are added, such as lighting fixtures and landscaping.

1.2.9 Final Inspections and Approvals

The home undergoes final inspections to ensure that it is safe and up to code. Approvals are obtained from local authorities to ensure that the home is legally compliant.

1.2.10 Moving In

Once the home is complete and approved, it's time to move in and start enjoying your dream home.

1.3 Choosing the Right Builder

Choosing the right builder is crucial to ensuring that your dream home is built to your specifications and with high-quality materials and workmanship. Here are a few factors to consider when choosing a builder:

1.3.1 Experience and Reputation

Look for a builder who has experience in the type of home you want to build and a strong reputation in the industry. Check online reviews and ask for references from previous clients.

1.3.2 Communication and Collaboration

Building a custom home requires collaboration between you and the builder. Look for a builder who is responsive to your needs and communicates clearly throughout the process.

1.3.3 Transparency and Pricing

A reputable builder will provide a clear and transparent pricing structure, including any additional costs that may arise during the building process.

1.3.4 Licensing and Insurance

Make sure that the builder you choose is licensed and insured to protect yourself in case of any accidents or issues during the building process.

1.3.5 Warranty and After-Sales Support

Find out what kind of warranty and after-sales support the builder offers. A builder who stands behind their work with a strong warranty and support system can give you peace of mind and protect your investment in your new home.

In conclusion, building your dream home is a complex process that requires careful planning, communication, and collaboration with a reputable builder. Understanding the building process and what to look for in a builder can help you turn your vision into a reality. In the following chapters, we'll dive deeper into each step of the building process and offer guidance on how to make the most of your custom home building experience.

Chapter 2: Establishing Your Needs and Wants

Building a custom home is a unique opportunity to create a living space that meets your specific needs and wants. In this chapter, we'll discuss how to establish your priorities for your dream home and how to ensure that the design and construction of your home reflects those priorities.

2.1 Understanding Your Lifestyle

The first step in establishing your needs and wants for your custom home is understanding your lifestyle. Think about how you and your family currently use your living space and what you would like to improve upon. Do you need more space for entertaining, a larger kitchen for cooking, or a dedicated home office? Consider how your lifestyle may change in the future, such as adding more children to your family or aging in place.

2.2 Creating a Wishlist

Once you have a clear understanding of your lifestyle needs, create a wishlist of features and amenities that you would like to incorporate into your dream home. This may include features such as a large master suite with a walk-in closet and ensuite bathroom, a chef's kitchen with top-of-the-line appliances, or a backyard pool and outdoor kitchen for entertaining. Don't forget to consider any unique features that may be specific to your interests or hobbies, such as a home theater or a dedicated yoga studio.

2.3 Prioritizing Your Wishlist

While it may be tempting to include all your wishlist items in your dream home, it's important to prioritize your needs and wants to ensure that your home is both functional and within your budget. Take some time to review your wishlist and rank each item in order of importance. Consider the frequency of use, the value it adds to your lifestyle, and the cost of including it in the design and construction of your home.

2.4 Balancing Design and Functionality

When designing your dream home, it's important to strike a balance between aesthetics and functionality. While you may have a specific design aesthetic in mind, it's important to ensure that the design elements you choose also serve a functional purpose. For example, incorporating ample storage solutions in your kitchen or incorporating a mudroom near the entrance can improve the functionality of your home while also contributing to its overall design.

2.5 Working with a Professional

Working with a professional architect or designer can help you to establish your needs and wants for your dream home and ensure that the design and construction reflect those priorities. A professional can offer guidance on design elements and materials that meet both your functional and aesthetic needs while also staying within your budget. They can also provide insights into emerging design trends and innovative technologies that can enhance the functionality and comfort of your home.

In conclusion, establishing your needs and wants for your custom home is an essential step in the planning process. By understanding your lifestyle, creating a wishlist, prioritizing your needs and wants, balancing design and functionality, and working with a professional, you can ensure that your dream home meets your specific needs and wants and reflects your unique personality and style. In the next chapter, we'll discuss the importance of selecting the right location for your custom home.

Chapter 3: Setting Your Budget

Building a custom home can be a dream come true for many individuals and families. However, it is important to realize that building a home is a significant financial investment. As such, it is essential to establish a realistic budget before beginning the building process. In this chapter, we will discuss the various costs associated with building a home, how to create a realistic budget, and provide tips for managing your budget throughout the building process.

3.1 Understanding the Costs Involved in Building a Home

Before creating a budget, it is important to have a clear understanding of the costs associated with building a home. The costs of building a home can vary widely depending on the size, location, design, and quality of materials used. Some of the major costs to consider include:

Land: The cost of purchasing land can vary significantly depending on the location, size, and zoning of the property. In some areas, land may be relatively inexpensive, while in others, it may be quite costly.

Materials: The cost of building materials can also vary depending on the quality and quantity of materials needed. Some materials, such as lumber and concrete, may be relatively inexpensive, while others, such as high-end finishes and appliances, can be quite costly.

Labor: The cost of labor will depend on the complexity of the project, the experience of the workers, and the location of the project. In some areas, labor costs may be relatively low, while in others, they may be quite high.

Permits and fees: Building permits and other fees associated with the building process can vary depending on your location. It is important to research the permit and fee requirements in your area and include them in your budget.

Design and engineering: The cost of designing and engineering your custom home will depend on the complexity of the project and the experience of the professionals you work with. It is important to work with experienced professionals who can help you design a home that meets your needs and budget.

It is important to research and estimate the costs associated with each of these components before setting your budget. This will help you to establish a realistic and achievable budget that reflects the true cost of building your dream home.

3.2 Establishing a Realistic Budget

Once you have a clear understanding of the costs involved in building a custom home, it is time to establish a realistic budget. Here are some tips on how to create a budget that is achievable:

Determine your overall budget: The first step in creating a budget is to determine your overall budget. This includes the maximum amount you are willing to spend on your custom home. It is important to be realistic about your budget and to consider all the costs associated with building your home.

Break down your budget: Once you have determined your overall budget, the next step is to break it down into categories such as land, materials, labor, design and engineering, permits and fees, and contingency funds. This will help you to better understand how your budget is allocated and identify areas where you may need to adjust your spending.

Allocate funds based on priorities: Use your wishlist from Chapter 2 to prioritize your needs and wants. Allocate funds to the areas of your home that are most important to you. For example, if you love to cook, you may want to allocate more funds to your kitchen than to other areas of your home.

Account for unexpected expenses: It is important to have a contingency fund in case unexpected expenses arise during the building process. Experts recommend setting aside 10-20% of your overall budget for unexpected expenses. This can help to ensure that you have the funds available to address any unforeseen issues that arise during the building process.

Consider financing options: If you need to finance your custom home, it is important to explore your options and to work with a lender who specializes in construction loans. Construction loans are typically short-term loans that provide funding during the building process. Once the home is completed, the construction loan is usually converted into a mortgage.

3.3 Managing Your Budget Throughout the Building Process

Creating a realistic budget is just the first step in building your dream home. It is important to manage your budget throughout the building process to ensure that you stay on track and avoid overspending. Here are some tips for managing your budget:

Communicate with your builder: It is important to have open and ongoing communication with your builder throughout the building process. This can help to ensure that there are no surprises and that everyone is on the same page when it comes to budget and expenses.

Track your expenses: Keep track of all your expenses throughout the building process. This will help you to stay on top of your budget and identify any areas where you may be overspending.

Make changes as needed: If unexpected expenses arise or you find that you are overspending in certain areas, be prepared to make changes to your budget. This may mean cutting back on expenses in other areas or finding creative solutions to stay within your budget.

Stick to your priorities: It can be tempting to add extra features or upgrades during the building process, but it is important to stick to your priorities and stay within your budget. Remember, you can always add upgrades and features later.

In conclusion, setting a realistic budget is an essential part of building your dream home. By understanding the costs associated with building a home, creating a realistic budget, and managing your budget throughout the building process, you can ensure that your dream home becomes a reality without breaking the bank.

Chapter 4: Financing Your Dream Home

Building your dream home is an exciting and rewarding process, but it can also be expensive. Financing your dream home can be a daunting task, but with the right knowledge and resources, you can make informed decisions that will help you achieve your goal of building the home of your dreams.

4.1 Understanding Your Financing Options

One of the most important aspects of financing your dream home is understanding your financing options. There are several options available, including construction loans, mortgages, and government-backed programs.

Construction Loans: A construction loan is a short-term loan that provides funding during the building process. These loans typically have higher interest rates and require a larger down payment than traditional mortgages. Once the home is completed, the construction loan is usually converted into a mortgage. It is important to note that construction loans are not always easy to obtain, as lenders will require detailed plans and specifications for the project, as well as a well-documented budget and timeline.

Mortgages: A mortgage is a long-term loan used to finance the purchase of a home. There are several types of mortgages available, including fixed-rate mortgages, adjustable-rate mortgages, and government-backed mortgages. Each type of mortgage has its own advantages and disadvantages, and it is important to research and compare different options to determine which one is right for you.

Fixed-rate mortgages offer a stable interest rate that does not change over the life of the loan. This can be beneficial for those who want predictable payments and do not want to worry about interest rate fluctuations. Adjustable-rate mortgages, on the other hand, have interest rates that can change over time. These mortgages often have lower initial interest rates than fixed-rate mortgages, but they can be riskier if interest rates rise in the future.

Government-Backed Programs: There are several government-backed programs available to help homebuyers finance their dream home. These include Federal Housing Administration (FHA) loans, Veterans Affairs (VA) loans, and United States Department of Agriculture (USDA) loans.

These programs often have lower down payment requirements and less stringent credit requirements than traditional mortgages, making them a great option for those who may not qualify for a traditional mortgage.

It is important to research and compare different financing options to determine which one is right for you. Consider factors such as interest rates, down payment requirements, and eligibility criteria when making your decision.

4.2 Getting Pre-Approved for a Mortgage

Once you have determined which financing option is right for you, it is important to get pre-approved for a mortgage. Pre-approval is a process in which a lender reviews your financial information and credit history to determine how much you can afford to borrow. This process can help you determine your budget and avoid any surprises during the building process.

To obtain pre-approval for a mortgage, you will need to provide documentation of your income, assets, and credit history. This information will be used to determine your creditworthiness and ability to repay the loan. It is important to note that pre-approval does not guarantee that you will be approved for a mortgage, but it can help you determine how much you can afford to borrow and what type of loan is best for your needs.

It is important to shop around and compare mortgage rates and terms from different lenders. This can help you find the best loan for your needs and budget. Be sure to read and understand the terms of the loan, including interest rates, fees, and repayment terms.

Once you have been pre-approved for a mortgage, it is important to stay within your budget and avoid taking on additional debt that could impact your ability to repay the loan. This may mean making sacrifices in other areas of your life, such as reducing expenses or delaying other purchases.

In conclusion, financing your dream home is a major decision that requires careful consideration and overall, financing a dream home can be a complex and overwhelming process. However, with careful planning, research, and the guidance of experienced professionals, it is possible to secure the financing needed to bring your dream home to life. By understanding your financing options, getting pre-approved for a mortgage, and working closely with a team of experts, you can ensure that the financing process runs smoothly and efficiently.

With the right financing in place, you can focus on the exciting journey of building your dream home and creating a space that truly reflects your unique style and personality.

Chapter 5: Finding a Building Site

Building a new home is a major investment that requires careful consideration and planning. One of the most crucial decisions to make is choosing the right location for your new home. In this chapter, we will guide you through the process of finding a building site that meets your needs and preferences. We'll explore the key factors to consider when selecting a location and discuss how to assess the suitability of a building site to ensure it is the right fit for your dream home.

Identifying Potential Locations for Your Home

Before you start your search for a building site, it's important to have a clear understanding of your needs and preferences. Consider your lifestyle and daily routine, as well as the location of your workplace, schools, and amenities that are important to you. If you have children, you may prioritize living in a good school district, while a retiree may seek a quiet, peaceful location. Some may want to be near public transportation, while others may prefer to be in a more rural area. It's important to take your time to identify your priorities and preferences, as this will guide your search and help you find a location that aligns with your vision for your dream home.

Once you have a clear idea of what you're looking for, it's time to start your search for potential locations. You can start by researching online, looking for listings on real estate websites, or reaching out to a local real estate agent. You can also drive around neighborhoods that interest you and look for "For Sale" signs or "Vacant Land" signs. By doing so, you'll start to get a sense of the neighborhoods that are available and which areas may be a good fit for your family.

When researching potential locations, consider factors such as proximity to your work, schools, and amenities such as parks, restaurants, and shopping centers. Think about your daily routine and how the location will impact your commute and lifestyle. In addition, research the crime rates in the area and talk to neighbors to get a sense of the community and its culture.

Assessing the Suitability of a Building Site

Once you've identified a few potential locations, the next step is to assess the suitability of each building site. This involves considering various factors such as the slope of the land, soil type, zoning regulations, and other potential site limitations.

Slope of the Land: One of the most important factors to consider is the slope of the land. A steep slope may require additional foundation work and grading, which can add to the cost of construction. A flat or gently sloping site is generally more desirable and easier to build on.

Soil Type: The type of soil on a building site can also impact the cost of construction. For instance, soil that is prone to erosion or expansive soils may require additional foundation work to ensure stability. It's important to have a soil analysis done to determine the suitability of the soil for construction.

Zoning Regulations: Zoning regulations vary by location, so it's important to research the regulations in the areas you're considering. These regulations may dictate the size and design of the home, as well as other restrictions such as setbacks and maximum building heights. It's important to work with a builder or architect who understands the local zoning regulations and can help you navigate any restrictions.

Other Site Limitations: Other potential site limitations may include easements, wetlands, and tree preservation ordinances. These factors may impact the design of your home and add to the cost of construction. It's important to work with a builder or architect who is familiar with these factors and can help you design a home that meets your needs while adhering to any site limitations.

In addition to assessing the suitability of a building site, it's also important to consider the long-term implications of the location. For instance, once a few potential locations have been identified, it's important to evaluate each one to determine its suitability for building. The following factors should be taken into consideration:

1. Soil Type: The soil type on the site can have a significant impact on the cost of building. For example, building on sandy soil may require additional foundation work to ensure stability, which can increase the overall cost of construction. It's important to conduct a soil test to determine the soil type and any necessary precautions or extra expenses.

2. Slope: The slope of a building site can also affect the cost of construction. Building on a

steep slope may require additional grading and excavation work to create a level building pad, which can increase the cost of construction.

3. Zoning Regulations: Local zoning regulations can dictate the size and placement of structures on a property. It's important to research the zoning laws in the area to ensure that the intended use and design of the property is allowed.

4. Environmental Considerations: Building on a site with sensitive environmental features, such as wetlands or endangered species, may require additional permits and approvals. It's important to evaluate any environmental concerns before purchasing a property to avoid delays and additional expenses.

5. Access: Consider how easy it is to access the site. Is it located on a main road or a quiet residential street? If the site is difficult to access, it may be more expensive to transport building materials and complete construction.

6. Utilities: Are utilities, such as water, sewer, and electricity, readily available on the site?

If not, connecting to these utilities can be a significant expense.

7. Neighborhood: Consider the character of the neighborhood and how it aligns with your lifestyle and preferences. Look at the surrounding homes and determine if they fit with your vision for your dream home.

Once these factors have been evaluated, it's important to narrow down the options and choose the best building site for your needs and budget.

It's important to note that finding the perfect building site can be a challenging and time-consuming process. However, taking the time to research and evaluate potential locations will help ensure that your dream home is built on a solid foundation. Working with a knowledgeable real estate agent or builder can also help make the process smoother and more efficient.

Chapter 6: Choosing a Builder

Choosing the right builder is one of the most important decisions you will make in the home building process. Your builder will be responsible for bringing your vision to life and ensuring that the project runs smoothly from start to finish. In this chapter, we'll provide guidance on how to evaluate potential builders and select the right builder for your project.

Evaluating Potential Builders

When evaluating potential builders, there are several key factors to consider. These include:

Reputation: A builder's reputation is perhaps the most important factor to consider when choosing a builder. Look for builders with a strong reputation for quality workmanship, timely delivery, and excellent customer service. Ask for references and check online reviews and ratings.

Experience: Look for builders with experience in the type of home you want to build. A builder who specializes in traditional homes may not be the best choice for a modern home, and vice versa. Ask about their experience with similar projects and for examples of their work.

Licenses and Insurance: Ensure that any builder you consider is licensed and insured in your state. This will protect you in case of any accidents or other issues during the construction process.

Communication: Communication is key when working with a builder. Look for a builder who is responsive to your calls and emails and who takes the time to understand your needs and concerns. Ask how they will keep you updated throughout the process and what methods of communication they prefer.

Budget and Timeline: Ask potential builders about their estimated budget and timeline for your project. Compare these with other builders and with your own budget and timeline to ensure that they are realistic and achievable.

Selecting the Right Builder for Your Project

Once you have evaluated potential builders, it's time to select the right builder for your project. This involves more than just choosing the builder with the lowest bid or the most experience. Here are some additional factors to consider:

Communication Style: Choose a builder who communicates in a way that you are comfortable with. Some builders may prefer to communicate primarily through email or phone calls, while others may prefer in-person meetings. Ensure that the builder's communication style aligns with your own.

Project Management: Ask potential builders about their project management process. Look for a builder who will be on-site regularly to ensure that the project is on track and who has a clear plan for handling any issues that may arise.

Shared Vision: Choose a builder who shares your vision for the project. This includes everything from the design and materials used to the overall style and feel of the home. Look for a builder who is willing to listen to your ideas and work with you to bring your vision to life.

Personality Fit: Finally, it's important to choose a builder who you feel comfortable working with. Building a home is a big project that can take months or even years to complete. Look for a builder who you feel you can trust and who you enjoy working with.

Conclusion

Choosing the right builder for your project is a crucial step in the home building process. Take the time to evaluate potential builders carefully and consider all the factors outlined in this chapter. By choosing a builder who is a good fit for your needs and preferences, you can ensure that your home building project is a success.

Chapter 7: Designing Your Home

Building a custom home allows you to create a space that is tailored to your needs, lifestyle, and aesthetic preferences. However, designing a custom home can be a complex and time-consuming process, and it's essential to work with an experienced architect or designer who can help you bring your vision to life. In this chapter, we will discuss the benefits of working with a professional designer, as well as offer guidance on how to create a custom home design that meets your needs and wants.

Working with an Architect or Designer

When it comes to designing a custom home, working with a professional architect or designer can make all the difference. These experts have the training and experience to take your ideas and translate them into a functional, aesthetically pleasing design that meets your specific requirements. They can also help you navigate the design process, providing guidance on everything from selecting materials to choosing fixtures and finishes.

There are many benefits to working with a professional designer. For one, they can help you stay within your budget by making recommendations for cost-effective materials and design features. They can also help you create a design that maximizes the use of natural light, energy-efficient features, and other eco-friendly solutions.

Another advantage of working with a designer is that they can help you navigate the complex world of building codes and regulations. They are familiar with local building codes and zoning requirements, ensuring that your design meets all the necessary criteria. This can save you time and money in the long run by avoiding costly fines or delays.

Choosing the Right Designer

Choosing the right designer is essential to the success of your custom home project. You want to work with someone who understands your vision and can translate it into a design that meets your needs and wants. Here are some tips for selecting the right designer for your project:

1. Ask for referrals: Ask friends, family, and other homeowners for recommendations for designers they have worked with in the past. You can also check online reviews and

ratings to get a sense of a designer's reputation.

2. Look at their portfolio: Review the designer's portfolio of past work to get a sense of their style and experience. Make sure their design aesthetic matches your vision for your custom home.

3. Conduct interviews: Once you have narrowed down your list of potential designers, schedule interviews to discuss your project and get a sense of their communication style and approach to the design process.

4. Check references: Ask for references from past clients and follow up with them to get a sense of their experience working with the designer.

Creating a Custom Home Design

Once you have selected a designer to work with, the next step is to create a custom home design that meets your needs and wants. Here are some tips for creating a successful design:

1. Identify your priorities: Start by identifying your priorities for your custom home, such as the number of bedrooms and bathrooms, the

layout of the living spaces, and any specific features or design elements you want to include.

2. Communicate your vision: Work closely with your designer to communicate your vision for your custom home. Provide as much detail as possible, including pictures, sketches, and other inspiration to help them understand your preferences.

3. Consider the site: Consider the characteristics of your building site, such as the slope, soil type, and zoning regulations, when designing your custom home. This can help you create a design that is well-suited to the site and meets all necessary requirements.

4. Make revisions as needed: The design process is iterative, and it's common to make revisions along the way. Work closely with your designer to review the design and make any necessary changes or adjustments to ensure it meets your needs and wants.

5. Think long-term: When designing your custom home, it's important to think about your long-term.

Overall, working with an architect or designer can be a valuable investment for anyone building a new home. By collaborating with a professional, homeowners can ensure that their home design is functional, aesthetically pleasing, and tailored to their specific needs and wants. With clear communication, flexibility, and patience, the design process can be an enjoyable and rewarding part of the home building journey.

In the next chapter, we'll explore the importance of obtaining necessary permits and approvals before beginning construction on your new home.

Chapter 8: Obtaining Permits and Approvals

Before beginning construction on your new home, it's important to obtain the necessary permits and approvals from local authorities. This process can be complex and time-consuming, but it's essential to ensure that your project follows local regulations and meets all safety and environmental standards. In this chapter, we'll discuss the permitting process and offer guidance on how to obtain necessary approvals to move forward with construction.

Understanding the Permitting Process

The permitting process can vary depending on the location of your building site and the type of construction project you're undertaking. However, there are some common steps and requirements that are typically involved in the process. Here are some of the key factors to consider:

Building Permits: Building permits are typically required for new construction, additions. These permits ensure that the construction meets all building codes and safety standards. To obtain a building permit, you'll need to submit detailed construction plans and pay a fee. The local building department will review your plans and may request revisions before approving the permit.

Zoning Permits: Zoning permits are required to ensure that the building project follows local zoning regulations. These regulations govern things like setback requirements, maximum building height, and land use restrictions. Zoning permits are typically issued by the local zoning board or planning commission.

Environmental Permits: Environmental permits may be required for building projects that could have an impact on the environment. This can include projects near wetlands, waterways, or other environmentally sensitive areas. To obtain an environmental permit, you'll need to submit a detailed environmental impact assessment and work with local environmental authorities to ensure that your project meets all requirements.

Obtaining Necessary Approvals from Local Authorities

To obtain necessary approvals from local authorities, it's important to be familiar with the permitting process and to work closely with your builder or contractor to ensure that all requirements are met. Here are some tips for navigating the process:

1. Research local regulations: Before beginning the permitting process, research the local regulations that govern building projects in your area. This can include building codes, zoning regulations, and environmental requirements. Work with your builder or architect to ensure that your project meets all necessary requirements.

2. Submit detailed plans: When applying for permits, submit detailed construction plans that clearly outline the scope of your project. This can include architectural drawings, engineering plans, and site plans. The more detail you provide, the easier it will be for local authorities to review your plans and approve your permits.

3. Be prepared to make revisions: Local authorities may request revisions to your plans before approving your permits. Be prepared to make necessary changes and work with your builder or architect to ensure that all requirements are met.

4. Pay attention to timelines: Permitting timelines can vary depending on the location and complexity of your project. Be sure to factor in permit processing times when creating your construction schedule. Delays in the permitting process can cause significant delays in your overall construction timeline.

5. Work with experienced professionals: To ensure that your project follows all regulations and requirements, work with experienced professionals, including builders, architects, and engineers. They can help guide you through the permitting process and ensure that all necessary approvals are obtained.

Conclusion

Obtaining necessary permits and approvals is a critical step in the home building process. By understanding the permitting process and working closely with local authorities and experienced professionals, you can ensure that your project meets all necessary requirements and is completed on time and on budget. Don't overlook the importance of obtaining necessary approvals - it can save you significant time and money in the long run.

Chapter 9: Preparing Your Building Site

Before construction can begin on your dream home, it's essential to prepare the building site properly. This chapter will discuss the various steps involved in site preparation, including clearing and grading the land and setting up a staging area for the construction process.

Clearing and Grading the Site

The first step in preparing your building site is to clear the land of any vegetation, trees, or debris that may obstruct the construction process. This process involves removing any existing structures, such as sheds or garages, and disposing of any unwanted materials. Once the site is clear, the land must be graded to create a level surface for the foundation and the construction process.

Grading the land involves using heavy equipment to level the ground and create a foundation that is both stable and properly sloped for drainage. This step is critical to ensure the long-term stability of your home's foundation and prevent water damage or erosion in the future.

Before beginning the grading process, it's important to consult with a professional contractor to assess the site's topography and soil conditions. This will ensure that the grading is done correctly and that any potential issues, such as drainage problems or soil instability, are addressed before construction begins.

Preparing for Construction

After the site has been cleared and graded, it's time to prepare for the start of construction. This involves setting up a temporary office and staging area to ensure that the construction process runs smoothly.

A temporary office is necessary to have a centralized location for all documentation, communication, and administrative tasks related to the construction process. The office should be equipped with all the necessary tools and equipment required to manage the project efficiently, including computers, phones, filing cabinets, and a secure storage space for important documents.

A staging area is another important component of site preparation. It's an area where materials, tools, and equipment can be stored and organized for easy access during construction. The staging area should be located near the site but out of the way of construction traffic to ensure safety and efficiency. It should also be equipped with a security system to protect the materials and equipment from theft or damage.

During the preparation phase, it's important to work with your builder or contractor to plan and coordinate the construction process. This includes establishing a timeline for the various stages of construction, setting realistic deadlines, and ensuring that all permits and approvals have been obtained before work begins.

In addition, it's important to ensure that the construction site is safe and secure for workers and visitors. This involves setting up safety protocols, such as erecting fencing around the site, posting warning signs, and providing safety equipment and training for workers.

Conclusion

Proper preparation of your building site is critical to ensuring the success of your construction project. From clearing and grading the land to setting up a temporary office and staging area, careful planning and coordination are essential to ensure that the construction process runs smoothly and efficiently.

Working with an experienced contractor or builder can help ensure that your building site is prepared correctly and that all necessary permits and approvals are obtained before construction begins. By following the guidelines outlined in this chapter, you can take the first step toward building your dream home on a stable and properly prepared site.

Chapter 10: Building the Foundation

Building a new home is an exciting and rewarding experience, but it can also be overwhelming at times. There are so many decisions to make, and one of the most important is the foundation. The foundation is the base upon which your entire home will rest, and it needs to be strong and stable to ensure the safety and longevity of your home. In this chapter, we will discuss the process of building the foundation and the different options available.

Pouring the Foundation

The first step in building a foundation is to pour the concrete slab. This is done by excavating the site to the appropriate depth and then pouring a layer of gravel or other material to provide a stable base. The concrete is then poured over the base and allowed to cure for several days. The process of pouring the concrete must be done correctly to ensure the foundation is level and strong.

One of the most important aspects of pouring a foundation is ensuring that it is level. If the foundation is not level, it can cause problems with the framing, windows, doors, and other elements of the home. To achieve a level foundation, builders will use a variety of tools, including laser levels and hand-held levels, to ensure the concrete is poured to the correct height and level.

Another key factor in pouring the foundation is the strength of the concrete. The concrete needs to be strong enough to support the weight of the home and withstand the forces of nature, such as earthquakes and high winds. Builders will often use reinforced concrete, which includes steel bars or mesh, to add strength to the foundation.

Constructing the Basement or Crawl Space

Once the foundation is poured and cured, the next step is to create the basement or crawl space. There are two main types of foundations: basement and crawl space. The choice between the two will depend on the site conditions and the homeowner's preferences.

Basement

A basement is a type of foundation that is built below ground level. It is typically used in areas with cold climates, where a basement can provide additional living space and protection from the elements. Building a basement involves creating walls and a floor that will support the weight of the home and provide a space for living or storage.

One of the advantages of a basement is the extra living space it provides. Homeowners can use the basement for a variety of purposes, such as a home theater, office, or extra bedroom. Another advantage is the protection it provides from severe weather, such as tornadoes or hurricanes. Basements can also be used as a shelter in case of emergency.

However, there are also some drawbacks to building a basement. One of the main drawbacks is the cost. Basements require more excavation, materials, and labor, which can add significantly to the cost of the home. Basements can also be prone to moisture problems, which can lead to mold and mildew if not properly addressed.

Crawl Space

A crawl space is a type of foundation that is built above ground level. It is typically used in areas with warmer climates, where a crawl space can provide ventilation and reduce the risk of moisture problems. Building a crawl space involves creating a raised floor and walls that will support the weight of the home.

One of the advantages of a crawl space is the lower cost compared to a basement. Crawl spaces require less excavation and materials, which can save homeowners money. Crawl spaces can also provide better ventilation and reduce the risk of moisture problems.

However, there are also some drawbacks to building a crawl space. One of the main drawbacks is the limited storage and living space it provides. Crawl spaces are typically only a few feet high, which makes it difficult to use the space for anything other than storage. Crawl spaces can also be prone to pest infestations if not properly sealed and maintained.

Conclusion

Once the foundation is poured and set, the next step is to start constructing the basement or crawl space. The choice between a basement or crawl space will depend on various factors, such as the type of soil, local building codes, and personal preferences.

A basement provides additional living space, storage, and protection against natural disasters, such as tornadoes and hurricanes. However, building a basement requires more excavation and construction work, which can add to the overall cost of the project.

On the other hand, a crawl space is typically less expensive to build and can provide easy access to plumbing and electrical systems. However, a crawl space may not be as suitable for storage or living space as a basement.

Regardless of the choice between a basement or crawl space, it is important to ensure proper waterproofing and ventilation to prevent moisture buildup and potential mold growth.

Overall, building the foundation is a critical step in the home-building process that requires careful planning, execution, and attention to detail. A solid foundation will ensure the stability and longevity of the home and provide a strong base for the rest of the construction process.

Chapter 11: Framing the House

Framing is one of the most critical components of home construction. The framing process involves creating the skeletal structure of the house, which will ultimately serve as the backbone for the entire building. The framing process typically involves the use of lumber, steel, or engineered wood products to create a framework that supports the entire building's weight. In this chapter, we will discuss the various aspects of the framing process, including types of framing, installation of windows and doors, and more.

Building the Frame of the Home The first step in the framing process is to construct the frame of the home. This process involves assembling the various components of the framing system, such as the floor joists, wall studs, and roof trusses. The frame of the home is the most crucial component of the building, as it provides the structure's support and stability.

The frame of the home is typically constructed using either wood or steel. Wooden frames are the most common choice for residential construction because they are readily available, easy to work with, and affordable. Steel frames are used in commercial and industrial buildings, and they offer significant benefits such as higher strength and durability. Regardless of the material chosen, the framing process typically involves the use of pre-cut framing members, which are then assembled on-site using nails, screws, or other fasteners.

Types of Framing There are two primary types of framing used in home construction: stick framing and panelized framing.

Stick framing, also known as traditional framing, involves constructing the home's frame on-site using individual pieces of lumber. This process involves cutting and assembling the various components of the frame, such as the wall studs, floor joists, and roof trusses. Stick framing is the most common type of framing used in residential construction because it is flexible and can accommodate custom designs.

Panelized framing, on the other hand, involves constructing the frame of the home in panels off-site, which are then transported to the building site and assembled. This method is becoming increasingly popular in residential construction due to its efficiency and cost-effectiveness. Panelized framing typically involves the use of computer-aided design (CAD) software to create precise panels that can be assembled quickly on-site.

Each type of framing has its advantages and disadvantages, and the choice between them ultimately depends on the specific needs and preferences of the homeowner.

Installing Windows and Doors Proper installation of windows and doors is crucial for ensuring energy efficiency, safety, and security. Windows and doors provide natural light, ventilation, and access to the outdoors. However, they can also be a significant source of energy loss if not installed correctly.

To ensure proper installation, windows and doors must be installed according to the manufacturer's specifications and industry best practices. This process involves framing the openings for the windows and doors, installing flashing to prevent water intrusion, and properly sealing the openings to prevent air leakage. The installation process also includes ensuring that the window and door frames are level and plumb, and that they operate smoothly.

There are several types of windows and doors available on the market, including casement windows, double-hung windows, sliding doors, and French doors. The choice between them depends on several factors, such as the style of the home, the amount of natural light desired, and the homeowner's preferences.

Conclusion The framing process is one of the most critical components of home construction. It involves constructing the frame of the home, which serves as the backbone for the entire building. The choice between stick framing and panelized framing depends on the homeowner's needs and preferences. Proper installation of windows and doors is also crucial for ensuring energy efficiency and safety. By understanding the framing process and its various components, homeowners can ensure that their new home is built to the highest standards of quality and safety.

Chapter 12: Electrical and Plumbing

Building a home involves a lot of moving parts, and among the most critical is the installation of electrical and plumbing systems. Electrical and plumbing work can be complicated, but understanding the process and choosing the right fixtures and appliances can help ensure that your home is safe, efficient, and functional.

Rough-in Electrical and Plumbing

The first step in electrical and plumbing installation is the rough-in, which happens before the walls are closed. During this phase, the electrician and plumber will run wires and pipes through the framing of the home to prepare for the installation of outlets, switches, and fixtures.

When it comes to electrical work, the rough-in phase includes installing the main service panel, wiring the outlets, and running cables to any switches, light fixtures, or other electrical components. This process also includes installing electrical boxes, which are the plastic or metal boxes that house the electrical connections and protect them from damage.

Similarly, rough-in plumbing involves running pipes and installing connectors for sinks, toilets, showers, and other water fixtures. The plumbing rough-in is a critical step that needs to be done right to avoid future problems like leaks or water damage.

Choosing Fixtures and Appliances

Once the rough-in phase is complete, it's time to start thinking about the fixtures and appliances that will be installed in the home. Choosing energy-efficient options is an excellent way to save money on utilities in the long run while also reducing your environmental impact.

When selecting fixtures, there are several factors to consider, such as water pressure, flow rate, and style. For example, a high-flow showerhead may feel luxurious, but it also uses more water than a low-flow option. Similarly, choosing faucets and toilets with a WaterSense label can help conserve water and reduce your monthly bill.

For appliances, look for models with the ENERGY STAR label, which indicates that they meet strict energy efficiency guidelines set by the U.S. Environmental Protection Agency (EPA). ENERGY STAR appliances are designed to use less energy and water, which can help reduce your utility bills and protect the environment.

In addition to choosing energy-efficient fixtures and appliances, it's also important to consider the overall design aesthetic of your home. For example, if you're going for a modern look, stainless steel appliances and sleek, minimalist fixtures might be the way to go. If you prefer a more traditional look, bronze or brass fixtures and appliances with more ornate details might be a better fit.

Working with a Professional

While it's possible to tackle electrical and plumbing work as a DIY project, it's generally recommended to hire a licensed professional to handle these tasks. Hiring a professional ensures that the work is done safely, efficiently, and up to code.

When choosing an electrician or plumber, do your research and check for licenses and certifications. You may also want to ask for references or look for reviews online to get a sense of the contractor's reputation.

It's also important to communicate your needs and preferences clearly to your electrician or plumber. This includes discussing your budget, design preferences, and any special needs or requirements you may have. Clear communication can help ensure that you get the results you want and avoid misunderstandings or mistakes.

Additionally, working with a professional can help ensure that your electrical and plumbing systems are properly integrated with the rest of your home's infrastructure. For example, an experienced electrician can help you design an electrical system that can handle the demands of your appliances and electronics, while a skilled plumber can ensure that your water pressure is consistent throughout the home.

Conclusion

Electrical and plumbing installation is a critical step in building a new home. Roughing in these systems and choosing the right fixtures and appliances can help ensure that your home is safe, efficient, and functional for years to come.

Chapter 13: Insulation and Drywall

As the construction of your dream home progresses, it's time to focus on insulation and drywall installation. These steps may not be as exciting as picking out paint colors or flooring, but they are crucial to the comfort, energy efficiency, and longevity of your new home. In this chapter, we'll discuss the importance of proper insulation, the various types of insulation, and how to ensure a smooth finish when hanging drywall.

Installing Insulation

Proper insulation is key to keeping your home comfortable and energy efficient. Without adequate insulation, heat can escape in the winter, and cool air can seep out during the summer. As a result, you're heating and cooling system must work harder to maintain a consistent temperature, leading to higher energy bills and potentially uncomfortable living conditions.

Insulation can also help reduce noise transmission between rooms and from outside. This is particularly important if you live in a noisy area or have a multi-story home where sound can easily travel between floors.

There are several types of insulation, each with its own set of benefits and drawbacks. The most common types of insulation used in residential construction are:

1. Fiberglass batt insulation: This is the most common type of insulation and is made of fine glass fibers. It comes in pre-cut batts or rolls and is relatively easy to install. Fiberglass insulation has a high R-value (which measures the insulation's ability to resist heat flow), making it an effective insulator. However, it can be irritating to the skin and lungs if inhaled and requires protective clothing and a respirator during installation.

2. Spray foam insulation: This type of insulation is sprayed into place and expands to fill gaps and crevices. Spray foam insulation has a high R-value and is an excellent air barrier, preventing air leaks and reducing energy loss. It's also water-resistant, making it a good choice for areas prone to moisture. However, it can be more expensive than other types of insulation and requires professional installation.

3. Cellulose insulation: Made of recycled paper and treated with chemicals to resist fire and pests, cellulose insulation is an eco-friendlier option. It has a high R-value and is relatively inexpensive compared to other types of insulation. However, it can settle over time, reducing its effectiveness, and requires specialized equipment for installation.

4. Mineral wool insulation: This type of insulation is made of rock or slag fibers and is known for its fire resistance and soundproofing capabilities. Mineral wool insulation has a high R-value and is resistant to mold and pests. However, it can be more expensive than other types of insulation and can be irritating to the skin and lungs if inhaled during installation.

When selecting insulation, consider factors such as the climate you live in, the location of your home, and your budget. Your builder or insulation contractor can help you determine the best type and amount of insulation for your home.

Hanging Drywall

Once the insulation is installed, it's time to move on to hanging drywall. This is an important step as it creates a smooth surface for painting or wallpapering and provides a fire-resistant barrier between rooms.

Here are the steps involved in hanging drywall:

1. Measure and cut the drywall: Measure the wall or ceiling where you'll be installing the drywall and use a utility knife to cut the drywall to size. Make sure to measure around any outlets, light switches, or vents.

2. Install the drywall: Position the drywall against the wall or ceiling and use drywall screws to secure it in place. Make sure to space the screws evenly and not too close to the edge of the drywall.

3. Tape the seams: Cover the seams between the drywall sheets with drywall tape, which helps prevent cracking.

After the insulation is installed, the next step is hanging drywall. Drywall, also known as gypsum board or sheetrock, is a common building material used to create walls and ceilings. It is a preferred option for its durability, versatility, and ease of installation.

The process of hanging drywall begins by measuring and cutting the sheets to fit the dimensions of the walls and ceilings. The sheets are then attached to the framing with screws or nails. It is essential to ensure that the drywall is installed evenly and with the right spacing between sheets to prevent cracking and warping.

After the drywall is installed, the seams and screw/nail holes are covered with joint compound and tape. This process is known as taping and finishing. The joint compound is applied to the seams and screw/nail holes and smoothed out with a drywall knife. Then, the tape is placed over the seams and smoothed out to remove any bubbles or wrinkles.

After the joint compound dries, it is sanded down to create a smooth surface. The process is repeated until the surface is even and ready for paint or wallpaper.

In addition to its aesthetic appeal, drywall also plays a crucial role in insulation. When properly installed, it can provide excellent soundproofing and thermal insulation, which can help reduce energy costs.

Overall, the installation of insulation and drywall is an essential part of the construction process. Proper insulation and drywall installation can help improve energy efficiency, provide a comfortable living space, and enhance the overall look and feel of your home. Working with experienced professionals can ensure that the process is done correctly and to the highest standards.

Chapter 14: Flooring, Painting, and Trim

After months of hard work, your dream home is starting to take shape. The framing, electrical, plumbing, and insulation are in place, and the walls are ready to be finished. The next step is to add the finishing touches that will turn your house into a home. In this chapter, we will discuss flooring, painting, and trim, three essential elements that will add style and personality to your new home.

Installing Flooring

Flooring is an essential part of any home, and it can make a significant impact on the overall look and feel of your space. Choosing the right flooring materials can be overwhelming, with so many options available in the market. From hardwood to tile, carpet to vinyl, the possibilities are endless. To choose the right flooring, it is important to consider your lifestyle, budget, and design preferences.

Hardwood flooring is a popular choice for its durability, beauty, and timeless appeal. It adds warmth and character to any room and can increase the value of your home. Hardwood flooring comes in a variety of species, grades, and finishes, and it can be stained to match your design preferences. It is important to choose a reputable installer to ensure that your hardwood floors are installed properly and will last for years to come.

Tile flooring is another popular option, especially in areas that experience high traffic or moisture, such as bathrooms and kitchens. Tile comes in a wide range of colors, patterns, and sizes, making it a versatile choice for any design style. It is durable, easy to clean, and can last for decades if properly installed and maintained.

Carpet is a comfortable and affordable option for bedrooms and living areas. It is available in a variety of colors and styles, from plush to low pile, and can add warmth and texture to any space. However, it is important to consider the maintenance requirements of carpet, as it can trap dirt and allergens and may need to be professionally cleaned on a regular basis.

Vinyl flooring is a durable and cost-effective option that can mimic the look of hardwood, tile, or stone. It is easy to install and maintain, making it a popular choice for busy households. It is available in a variety of colors and styles, from classic to contemporary, and can be a great option for kitchens, bathrooms, and basements.

No matter what flooring material you choose, it is important to hire a professional installer to ensure that it is installed properly. A poorly installed floor can not only look unattractive but can also pose safety hazards and decrease the value of your home.

Choosing Paint Colors

Painting is an easy and affordable way to add color and personality to your new home. Choosing the right paint colors can be overwhelming, with thousands of options available in the market. To narrow down your choices, it is important to consider your design style, the lighting in your space, and the mood you want to create.

Neutral colors are a popular choice for their versatility and timeless appeal. Shades of white, beige, gray, and taupe can create a calm and soothing atmosphere, and they can complement any design style. They also provide a neutral backdrop for artwork, furniture, and accessories.

Bold colors are a great option for adding personality and drama to your space. Reds, blues, greens, and yellows can create a vibrant and energetic atmosphere, and they can be used to highlight architectural features or create an accent wall. It is important to use bold colors sparingly and to balance them with neutral or complementary hues.

Pastel colors are a popular choice for creating a soft and romantic atmosphere. Light pinks, blues, and greens can add a touch of whimsy and charm to your space and can be used in bedrooms, bathrooms, and nurseries.

Once the trim is installed, the home will begin to take on a more polished look. Homeowners can select from a variety of materials for their trim, such as wood or composite materials. The most popular types of trim include baseboards, crown molding, window and door casings, and chair rails.

Baseboards are installed at the bottom of walls to cover the joint between the wall and the floor. They come in a variety of styles and sizes and can be painted or stained to match the floor or other trim in the home. Crown molding is installed where the wall meets the ceiling and adds a decorative touch to the room. Window and door casings are used to frame the openings of windows and doors and can be designed to match the style of the home. Chair rails are installed at the height of a chair back and are often used in dining rooms or other areas where furniture may come into contact with the walls.

It is important to hire a professional to install the trim in your home, as improper installation can lead to unsightly gaps or unevenness. A skilled carpenter can ensure that the trim is installed correctly and that the joints are tight and smooth. They can also offer advice on selecting the best materials for your needs and budget.

In conclusion, the flooring, painting, and trim stages of home construction are crucial for achieving the desired look and feel of the home. Homeowners should take the time to carefully consider their options and hire professionals to ensure that the work is done correctly. By doing so, they can create a beautiful and functional space that they can enjoy for years to come.

Chapter 15: Cabinets and Countertops

In this chapter, we will discuss different options for cabinetry and countertops, including custom or prefabricated, and how to choose the best option for your needs. We will also discuss the importance of selecting the right countertop materials and ensuring proper installation.

Choosing Cabinets

When it comes to selecting cabinets, there are many options available, including custom or prefabricated. Let's take a closer look at each option.

Custom Cabinets

Custom cabinets are built to the specific requirements of a homeowner. These cabinets are created by skilled carpenters who have the expertise to design and build cabinets that meet your exact needs. Custom cabinets offer a high level of flexibility in terms of design, materials, and finishes. They are also made from high-quality materials, ensuring that they will last for many years to come.

One of the main benefits of custom cabinets is that they offer a high level of customization. You can choose the exact size and shape of the cabinets, as well as the type of wood and finish. This level of customization is not possible with prefabricated cabinets.

However, custom cabinets are more expensive than prefabricated cabinets. The cost of custom cabinets can be up to three times more than the cost of prefabricated cabinets. Additionally, custom cabinets take longer to build, so you will need to plan for a longer lead time.

Prefabricated Cabinets

Prefabricated cabinets are pre-built and come in standard sizes. These cabinets are mass-produced, making them less expensive than custom cabinets. Prefabricated cabinets are available in a variety of styles, finishes, and colors, making it easy to find the right cabinets for your needs.

One of the main benefits of prefabricated cabinets is that they are readily available. You can walk into a home improvement store and purchase prefabricated cabinets off the shelf. Prefabricated cabinets are also easy to install, making them a popular choice for homeowners who want to save money on installation costs.

However, prefabricated cabinets offer less flexibility in terms of customization. You cannot change the size or shape of the cabinets, and you are limited in terms of the type of wood and finish you can choose.

How to Choose the Best Option for Your Needs

When choosing between custom or prefabricated cabinets, it is essential to consider your budget, timeline, and design preferences. Here are a few things to keep in mind:

1. Budget - Custom cabinets are more expensive than prefabricated cabinets. If you have a limited budget, prefabricated cabinets may be the better option.

2. Timeline - Custom cabinets take longer to build than prefabricated cabinets. If you have a tight timeline, prefabricated cabinets may be the better option.

3. Design preferences - If you have a specific design in mind that requires customization, then custom cabinets may be the better option. However, if you are happy with a standard design, prefabricated cabinets may be the better option.

Selecting Countertops

Selecting the right countertop is crucial for the overall look and feel of your kitchen or bathroom. Countertops are available in a variety of materials, including granite, quartz, marble, and laminate. Let's take a closer look at each material.

Granite Countertops

Granite countertops are a popular choice for homeowners. Granite is a natural stone that is durable and resistant to scratches, stains, and heat. Granite countertops come in a variety of colors and patterns, making it easy to find the right one for your kitchen or bathroom.

One of the main benefits of granite countertops is their durability. Granite countertops can last for many years if properly maintained. They are also heat resistant, which means that you can place hot pans and pots on them without worrying about damaging the surface.

However, granite countertops can be expensive, and the cost can vary depending on the type of granite you choose. Additionally, granite countertops require regular maintenance, including sealing, to keep them in good condition.

Quartz Countertops

Quartz countertops are another popular option for homeowners. Quartz is a man-made material made from crushed stone and resin. Quartz countertops are durable, easy to maintain, and come in a variety of colors and patterns.

One of the main benefits of quartz countertops is their durability. Quartz countertops are resistant to scratches, stains, and heat, making them an excellent choice for high-traffic areas such as kitchens and bathrooms. Quartz countertops are also easy to clean and require little maintenance.

However, quartz countertops can be more expensive than other materials, such as laminate. Additionally, quartz countertops can be damaged by heat, so it is essential to use trivets or hot pads when placing hot items on the surface.

Marble Countertops

Marble countertops are a classic choice for homeowners. Marble is a natural stone that is known for its beauty and elegance. Marble countertops come in a variety of colors and patterns, making them an excellent choice for homeowners who want a unique and stylish look.

One of the main benefits of marble countertops is their beauty. Marble countertops are elegant and timeless, and they can add value to your home. Additionally, marble is heat resistant, making it a great choice for high-traffic areas such as kitchens.

However, marble countertops are not as durable as other materials, such as granite or quartz. Marble countertops are susceptible to scratches and stains, and they require regular maintenance, including sealing.

Laminate Countertops

Laminate countertops are an affordable option for homeowners. Laminate is a synthetic material that is made from paper or fabric that is impregnated with resin and covered with a layer of plastic. Laminate countertops come in a variety of colors and patterns, making it easy to find the right one for your kitchen or bathroom.

One of the main benefits of laminate countertops is their affordability. Laminate countertops are much less expensive than other materials, such as granite or quartz. Additionally, laminate countertops are easy to clean and require little maintenance.

However, laminate countertops are not as durable as other materials, such as granite or quartz.

Laminate countertops can be scratched and damaged easily, and they are not heat resistant.

How to Ensure Proper Installation

Proper installation is essential to the longevity and functionality of your countertops. Here are a few things to keep in mind when installing countertops:

1. Hire a Professional - It is essential to hire a professional to install your countertops. A professional installer will have the expertise and tools to install your countertops properly.

2. Measure Carefully - It is crucial to measure your countertops carefully to ensure a proper fit. Make sure to measure the space accurately, including any cut-outs for sinks or appliances.

3. Choose the Right Material - Make sure to choose the right material for your needs. Some materials, such as granite or quartz, require extra support, so it is essential to factor this into your installation plans.

4. Follow Manufacturer Guidelines - It is important to follow the manufacturer's guidelines for installation, including any recommended adhesives or sealants.

Conclusion

In conclusion, cabinets and countertops are essential features in any kitchen or bathroom. When choosing cabinets, it is essential to consider your budget, timeline, and design preferences. Custom cabinets offer more flexibility in terms of customization, while prefabricated cabinets are more readily available and less expensive.

Chapter 16: Final Touches

The final touches of a home project can make a significant impact on the overall look and feel of the space. Whether you are renovating a kitchen, bathroom, or entire home, the final touches, including lighting fixtures and landscaping, are essential to creating a finished and polished look.

Installing Lighting Fixtures

Proper lighting is essential in any home project. The right lighting can enhance the look and feel of a space, while also providing functionality and safety. When selecting lighting fixtures for your project, it is essential to consider your style and budget.

Types of Lighting Fixtures

There are many types of lighting fixtures to choose from, including:

1. Pendant Lights - Pendant lights are a popular choice for kitchen islands and dining areas. They come in a variety of styles and sizes, making it easy to find the right one for your space.

2. Chandeliers - Chandeliers are a classic lighting fixture that can add elegance and

sophistication to any space. They come in a variety of styles and sizes, making it easy to find the right one for your home.

3. Recessed Lighting - Recessed lighting is a popular choice for bathrooms and kitchens. They provide bright and even lighting, making it easy to see while performing tasks.

4. Wall Sconces - Wall sconces are a great choice for bedrooms and bathrooms. They provide soft and warm lighting, making it easy to relax and unwind.

5. Table Lamps - Table lamps are a great way to add warmth and ambiance to any space. They come in a variety of styles and sizes, making it easy to find the right one for your home.

Choosing the Right Lighting Fixture

When selecting lighting fixtures for your project, it is essential to consider your style and budget. Here are a few things to keep in mind when selecting lighting fixtures:

1. Consider the Style - Lighting fixtures come in a variety of styles, from modern to traditional. Make sure to choose a fixture that fits the overall style of your home.

2. Consider the Size - Lighting fixtures come in a variety of sizes, so make sure to choose a fixture that is proportionate to the size of your room.

3. Consider the Budget - Lighting fixtures can vary in price, so make sure to choose a fixture that fits your budget.

4. Consider the Functionality - Make sure to choose a fixture that provides the right amount of light for the space. For example, recessed lighting is great for task lighting in the kitchen, while table lamps are perfect for creating a warm and cozy atmosphere in the living room.

Landscaping

Landscaping is an essential part of creating a welcoming and attractive outdoor space. Whether you are renovating the interior or exterior of your home, landscaping can add value and curb appeal to your property.

Types of Landscaping

There are many types of landscaping to choose from, including:

1. Trees and Shrubs - Trees and shrubs can add color and texture to your landscaping. They also provide privacy and shade, making them a great choice for any property.

2. Flowers - Flowers are a great way to add color and fragrance to your landscaping. They come in a variety of colors and sizes, making it easy to find the right ones for your property.

3. Hardscaping - Hardscaping includes elements such as patios, walkways, and retaining walls. These elements can add structure and functionality to your outdoor space.

4. Water Features - Water features such as fountains, ponds, and waterfalls can add a peaceful and calming element to your outdoor space.

Choosing the Right Landscaping

When selecting landscaping for your property, it is essential to consider your style and budget. Here are a few things to keep in mind when selecting landscaping

1. Consider the Climate - Make sure to choose landscaping that is appropriate for your

climate. For example, if you live in a dry climate, you may want to choose plants that are drought resistant.

2. Consider the Maintenance - Make sure to choose landscaping that is easy to maintain. For example, if you do not have a lot of time to devote to gardening, you may want to choose plants that require minimal upkeep.

3. Consider the Functionality - Make sure to choose landscaping that is functional for your needs. For example, if you have children or pets, you may want to choose landscaping that provides a safe and secure area for them to play.

4. Consider the Overall Design - Make sure to choose landscaping that fits the overall design of your property. For example, if you have a modern home, you may want to choose landscaping that has a sleek and contemporary look.

Ensuring Proper Installation

Proper installation is essential for both lighting fixtures and landscaping. Improper installation can lead to safety hazards and costly repairs down the line. Here are a few tips to ensure proper installation:

1. Hire a Professional - Hiring a professional can ensure that your lighting fixtures and landscaping are installed correctly. They have the knowledge and experience needed to ensure a safe and functional installation.

2. Follow the Manufacturer's Instructions - Make sure to follow the manufacturer's instructions when installing lighting fixtures and landscaping. This will ensure that they are installed correctly and function properly.

3. Check Local Codes and Regulations - Make sure to check local codes and regulations when installing lighting fixtures and landscaping. This will ensure that you are following any safety or zoning requirements.

4. Regular Maintenance - Regular maintenance is essential for both lighting fixtures and landscaping. Make sure to clean and inspect them regularly to ensure that they are functioning properly and looking their best.

Conclusion

The final touches of a home project can make a significant impact on the overall look and feel of the space. Proper lighting and landscaping can enhance the functionality and aesthetics of both the interior and exterior of your home. By selecting the right lighting fixtures and landscaping and ensuring proper installation, you can create a finished and polished look for your home project.

Chapter 17: Final Inspections and Approvals

After a long and often challenging process of renovating a home, the final stage is to obtain the necessary inspections and approvals to ensure the home is safe, up to code, and legally compliant. This chapter will cover the importance of final inspections and the process of obtaining final approvals from local authorities.

Final Inspections

The final inspections are crucial to ensure that the home project has been completed safely and up to code. Final inspections are typically performed by local building officials, and they will check the entire project to ensure that it meets all the required building codes and regulations.

The importance of final inspections cannot be overstated. Building codes are in place to protect the health, safety, and welfare of the public. They are designed to ensure that structures are safe, secure, and comply with all relevant regulations. Final inspections provide an opportunity for building officials to ensure that all work has been completed correctly and that the home is safe for occupancy.

During the final inspection, the building official will examine all aspects of the project, including the plumbing, electrical systems, HVAC, and structural components. They will check for proper installation, adequate support, and compliance with building codes and regulations.

If the inspector finds any issues during the final inspection, the contractor will be required to address them before the home is approved for occupancy. This can include anything from minor repairs to major structural modifications.

Obtaining Final Approvals

Once the final inspection has been completed and any necessary repairs have been made, the next step is to obtain final approvals from the local authorities. This process can vary depending on your location, but generally involves applying and paying a fee to the appropriate agency.

The final approval process is designed to ensure that the home project meets all the legal requirements for occupancy. This includes compliance with zoning laws, building codes, and other regulations that are in place to ensure that the home is safe and secure.

To obtain final approvals, you will need to provide documentation that demonstrates compliance with all relevant regulations. This may include building plans, permits, and inspection reports. You may also need to provide evidence of compliance with zoning laws, such as proof of setbacks, lot coverage, or other zoning requirements.

Once you have submitted your application and provided all the necessary documentation, the agency will review your application and schedule a final inspection. If everything is in order, the agency will issue a certificate of occupancy, which indicates that the home is legally compliant and safe for occupancy.

Conclusion

The final inspections and approvals are an essential part of the home process. They ensure that the home is safe and compliant with all relevant regulations and provide peace of mind for homeowners and occupants. It is important to work closely with building officials and other local authorities to ensure that all required inspections and approvals are obtained in a timely and efficient manner. By doing so, you can be confident that your home project has been completed to the highest standards of safety and quality.

Chapter 18: Moving In

Congratulations! You've made it to the final stage of your home project. It's time to move in and start enjoying your newly renovated home. In this chapter, we'll offer guidance on moving in and settling into your new home, including organizing and unpacking.

Moving In

Moving can be a stressful and overwhelming experience, especially after completing a major home project. However, with proper planning and preparation, you can make the process as smooth and stress-free as possible.

One of the first steps in the moving process is to create a moving plan. This plan should include a timeline, budget, and list of tasks that need to be completed before and after the move. You should also consider hiring professional movers to help you with the heavy lifting and transportation of your belongings.

Before you start packing, it's important to declutter and organize your belongings. This can help you to reduce the number of items you need to move, and make it easier to unpack and organize your new home. Sort your belongings into categories, such as keep, donate, sell, or toss, and be ruthless about getting rid of items that you no longer need or use.

Packing can be a time-consuming task, so start as early as possible. Use sturdy boxes and packing materials, and label each box with its contents and the room it belongs in. This can make the unpacking process much easier, as you can easily locate the items you need in each room.

Settling In

Once you've moved into your new home, it's time to start settling in. This process can take some time, but it's important to take it slow and enjoy the process of making your new house feel like a home.

One of the first things you should do is to unpack and organize your belongings. Start with the essentials, such as bedding, kitchenware, and bathroom supplies, and work your way through the rest of your boxes. As you unpack, take the time to assess your storage needs and consider adding additional storage solutions if necessary.

Next, take the time to familiarize yourself with your new home. Walk around and explore each room and take note of any features or issues that may need attention. Make a list of any repairs or upgrades that you would like to make in the future.

It's also important to take care of any maintenance tasks that may need to be done. Change the locks, check the smoke detectors, and make sure that the utilities are set up correctly. This can help to ensure that your home is safe and comfortable to live in.

Finally, take the time to decorate and personalize your new space. Hang pictures, add decorative accents, and choose furniture that reflects your personal style and needs. This can help to create a warm and inviting atmosphere in your new home.

Conclusion

Moving into a newly renovated home can be a rewarding and exciting experience. However, it can also be stressful and overwhelming. By following the tips and guidelines in this chapter, you can make the moving process as smooth and stress-free as possible.

Remember to create a moving plan, declutter and organize your belongings, and take your time settling in. With proper planning and preparation, you can create a beautiful and functional living space that you will be proud to call your own.

Chapter 19: Maintaining Your Dream Home

You've invested a lot of time and money into your new dream home, and now it's important to keep it in good condition. Regular maintenance and timely repairs can help to prevent costly damage and ensure that your home remains safe, comfortable, and beautiful for years to come. In this chapter, we'll discuss the importance of regular maintenance tasks and offer advice on scheduling repairs and upgrades.

Regular Maintenance Tasks

Regular maintenance tasks are essential for keeping your home in good condition. These tasks include cleaning gutters, changing HVAC filters, and checking for leaks. By performing these tasks on a regular basis, you can prevent damage to your home and ensure that it remains safe and comfortable for you and your family.

One of the most important regular maintenance tasks is cleaning gutters. Gutters are designed to collect and redirect rainwater away from your home, but they can become clogged with leaves, dirt, and other debris over time. This can cause water to overflow and damage your home's foundation, siding, and landscaping. To prevent this, it's important to clean your gutters at least twice a year, or more frequently if you live in an area with heavy rainfall or lots of trees.

Another important maintenance task is changing HVAC filters. HVAC filters help to keep your home's air clean and healthy by trapping dust, pollen, and other allergens. Over time, these filters can become clogged, which can reduce the efficiency of your HVAC system and cause it to work harder than necessary. To prevent this, it's important to change your filters every 1-3 months, depending on the type of filter and your home's usage.

Checking for leaks is also an important regular maintenance task. Leaks can occur in your plumbing, roofing, or windows, and can cause damage to your home's structure and interior. To prevent this, it's important to check for leaks on a regular basis, especially after heavy rainfall or strong winds. Look for water stains on your ceilings or walls and check your windows and doors for drafts.

Scheduling Repairs and Upgrades

In addition to regular maintenance tasks, it's important to schedule repairs and upgrades as needed to keep your home in good condition. Some repairs and upgrades may be necessary to prevent damage or ensure the safety of your home, while others may be cosmetic or functional upgrades to improve your home's value and comfort.

When scheduling repairs and upgrades, it's important to prioritize your needs and budget accordingly. Start by making a list of repairs and upgrades that you would like to make, and then prioritize them based on their importance and cost. Consider hiring a professional home inspector or contractor to assess your home's condition and provide recommendations on repairs and upgrades.

Some common repairs and upgrades include:

Roof repairs or replacement: A damaged or leaky roof can cause extensive damage to your home's structure and interior. If you notice signs of damage or wear, such as missing shingles or water stains on your ceiling, it's important to schedule a roof repair or replacement as soon as possible.

Plumbing repairs: Leaky pipes, clogged drains, and other plumbing issues can cause water damage and increase your water bill. If you notice any signs of plumbing issues, such as low water pressure or slow draining sinks, it's important to schedule a plumbing repair as soon as possible.

Energy-efficient upgrades: Energy-efficient upgrades can help to reduce your energy bills and improve your home's value and comfort. Consider upgrading your windows, insulation, or HVAC system to improve your home's energy efficiency.

Cosmetic upgrades: Cosmetic upgrades, such as painting, landscaping, or new flooring, can improve your home's value and comfort. Consider scheduling these upgrades based on your budget and timeline.

Conclusion

Maintaining your dream home requires regular maintenance tasks and timely repairs and upgrades. By staying on top of these tasks, you can prevent damage to your home and ensure that it remains safe, comfortable, and beautiful for years to come. Remember to prioritize your needs and budget when scheduling repairs and upgrades, and don't hesitate to seek the advice of professionals when needed. With proper maintenance and care, your dream home will continue to be a source of pride and comfort for you and your family.

Chapter 20: Conclusion

Building a dream home is an exciting and challenging process that requires careful planning, attention to detail, and a willingness to adapt and overcome obstacles. From the initial concept and design to the final inspection and move-in, building a dream home is a journey that can be both rewarding and stressful.

Looking back on the process, it's clear that building a dream home is not for the faint of heart. It requires a significant investment of time, money, and effort, and there are many decisions to be made along the way. From choosing the right location and design to selecting the right contractors and materials, every step of the process requires careful consideration and planning.

Despite the challenges, building a dream home is a journey that can be incredibly rewarding. There is nothing quite like the feeling of walking into a home that you have designed and built from the ground up, knowing that every detail has been chosen to meet your specific needs and preferences. Whether it's a custom kitchen, a luxurious master suite, or a backyard oasis, your dream home reflects your personality and style, and it's something to be proud of.

Of course, the journey to building your dream home is not without its challenges. There will be setbacks and unexpected expenses along the way, and it's important to stay flexible and open to change. At times, it may feel overwhelming, but by staying focused on your goals and working with a team of trusted professionals, you can overcome any obstacles and create a home that truly reflects your vision and style.

Now that your dream home is complete, it's time to enjoy the fruits of your labor. Take time to explore your new home and appreciate all the little details that make it special. Celebrate with family and friends and take pride in the accomplishment of building your dream home. You've worked hard to create a space that is uniquely yours, and now it's time to enjoy it to the fullest.

Of course, building your dream home is not the end of the journey. As with any home, there will be maintenance and repairs to consider, and it's important to stay on top of these tasks to ensure that your home remains safe and comfortable for years to come. But with proper care and attention, your dream home will continue to be a source of pride and comfort for you and your family for many years to come.

In conclusion, building a dream home is a journey that requires dedication, hard work, and a willingness to embrace change. But with the right team of professionals, careful planning, and a focus on your goals, you can create a space that truly reflects your vision and style. Enjoy your new home and take pride in the accomplishment of building your dream home.

Legal Disclaimer:

The information provided by this service is for general informational purposes only and is not intended to be, nor should it be construed as, legal or financial advice. The content provided is not a substitute for professional legal or financial advice.

Although we strive to provide accurate and up-to-date information, we make no representations or warranties of any kind, express or implied, about the completeness, accuracy, reliability, suitability or availability with respect to the website or the information, products, services, or related graphics contained on the website for any purpose. Any reliance you place on such information is therefore strictly at your own risk.

In no event will we be liable for any loss or damage including without limitation, indirect or consequential loss or damage, or any loss or damage whatsoever arising from loss of data or profits arising out of, or in connection with, the use of this service.

It is always recommended to seek professional legal or financial advice before making any decisions that may have legal or financial consequences.

www.ingramcontent.com/pod-product-compliance
Lightning Source LLC
Chambersburg PA
CBHW070607220526
45467CB00003B/1333